ACCRETION

APR. 23, 2020

ACCRETION

IRFAN ALI

Brick Books

Library and Archives Canada Cataloguing in Publication

Title: Accretion / Irfan Ali.
Names: Ali, Irfan, 1985– author.
Description: Poems.
Identifiers: Canadiana (print) 20190238208 | Canadiana (ebook) 20190238216 |
    ISBN 9781771315180 (softcover) | ISBN 9781771315197 (HTML) |
    ISBN 9781771315203 (PDF)
Classification: LCC PS8601.L415 A73 2020 | DDC C811/.6—dc23

We acknowledge the Canada Council for the Arts, the Government of Canada
through the Canada Book Fund, and the Ontario Arts Council for their support of
our publishing program.

The author photo was taken by Sarah Bodri.
The book is set in Proxima Nova.

Design and layout by Marijke Friesen.
Cover design by Rizwan Ali.
Printed and bound by Coach House Printing.

Brick Books
115 Haliburton Road
London, ON
N6K 2Z2

www.brickbooks.ca

For my mother Najma,
who taught me life can take root anywhere,
even in a desert.

CONTENTS

Bismillah hir-Rahman nir-Rahim.

In the name of God,
the Most Gracious, the Most Merciful.

ORIGINS

RECKLESS ABANDON

Spend long enough in the gutter
and you're bound to hear an old cosmic joke:
a boy crafted by loving hands
but imbued with fire
is deposited into a desert.
So, like a sadder Midas,
all he grasps for
turns to ash.

It's the heretic
I've tried to keep at bay who tells it,
even when two towers fell
and it was safe to turn apostate.
It's the heretic who tells it,
usurping me cell by cell,
until now when barely
enough remains to resist.

This is it then,
my farewell salaah,
my final prayer.

If You're there then,
prove Yourself different
from the old deities
known first for their flaws.
Dam up this dusty river, divert
me from this course where
I meet Your angels for judgment
and decline the infirmary's mercy.

I recline in the defendant's box
with my legs up,
proudly picking every wound.

I mock the roll call of my sins
until even the demons gasp
at my petulance.
A child given so much.
A child so fully abandoned.

MOTHER,

Maybe it's the lot of all mothers
to suffer this,
to offer their dreams and hopes
to other mouths
and abandon any claim
to recompense.

Even now I'm amazed
how your hands refuse to tremble
through every disappointment
and every failure, I am
amazed beyond all understanding.

How can there be so much love here?
How
        can there even be any?

FATHER,

At the bottom of a cup of tea
or in the entrails of a sacrificial goat,
a prophecy must have seeded a fear in you,
not unlike what came to Zeus
or his father Cronos before him.

But father, by now you must know
the age of prophecy is over.
There will be no answers in the fatty skins
that settled over last night's chai.
You will find no mercy
at the end of all your tear-stained prayers.

Father, now there is only
the possibility of forgiveness
and the lingering threat of the you in me
that still wants to watch you burn.

FOUR SONS

Even mom thinks we'll never make it,
some permutation of four
doomed to channel Cain.

The best we'll aspire to,
a vow of silence:

Go on your ways,
in peace and in pain.

Go,
with your backs squared
from our cruel tutelage,
and I will do the same.

SONG FOR MY SISTERS

You were two I think,
only beans in this world
but women in another.

Who were to be the coaches
through my clumsy games,
or the mortar binding tradition
to honour.

Love is an unbreachable mass,
Mama taught me.
It's only moved
from one place to another.

You'd both already taken root.

To be part sister
in a brother's body
is a special kind of cruelty.
But in a world already burning
with what it means to be a man,
maybe that
is the only mercy.

PAKI

means pure.
So it's strange how any white boy
could pry it from my hands
and wield it against me.

Maybe the scars can explain it, left
as they cracked and cracked our nations open
to slake their thirsts.
Or it's that promise that even now hangs
at the end of every sentence.

But purity is meant first as an armour.

A people lifted us up
on the crest of their dreams.
Sent us to sanctuary
and in return
asked only to be remembered.

Maybe the word cuts
because it's an empty promise,
like a man who still proclaims the Shahada
though he's long ago abandoned the faith.

Why didn't they choose another
to ward over their memory?
Couldn't my forebears tell I was a coward?
That I'd forget all of their faces?
That I'd be so wounded by a single word?

CEASEFIRES

Signed here
at shift changes and bus stops,
by hands fighting the urge to be fists.

They watched as we grew here
on the other side of a divide,
little aliens
making friends and lovers
of old enemies and overseers.

A history
of violence is still
a history.

For us, a new terror:
this gaping unknown they call Toronto,
our patron saint of fear,
our limbo of lost lovers –
through that darkened pine forest
we forge alone
along an unworn path.

COWARDS IN LOVE

There is love, then there's the other thing:
freezing with fear before you're halfway in.

Our imam can't tell the difference.
In his eyes all flesh leads into flame.

Our elders should've found us better teachers.
What is faith but the path between lovers' games?

We're powerless to avoid them either.
Boys like us have less agency than angels even.

REFLECTION

LAYLA

This is the story of two stars
and their long, solitary hurtlings.

He, an anomaly unmoored
within the cosmic barren,
silently accreting but secretly desperate
for the pull of other gravities.
It's then he sights her
growing against the horizon,
a bloom who makes
a barren burn more brilliant.

This is the imperceptible arc of fate.
The inevitability of attaining orbit.

But no binary system
is ever truly stable.

WATER

Like Narcissus, you could let yourself
waste away on the bank.
Some questions
are more important than survival.

What is it there
dancing beyond the surface?
Reflection or refraction?
The self or the fantasy?

A SEEING

The panicked first moment
like an echo's echo
from a long-forsaken cave,
an endless cascade
across a hall of mirrors,
unmistakable even
if the collision had
left me blind.

ENDOCYTOSIS

Her hands were protean things,
marvels beyond form or function.

And when they closed around mine,
they left no room for words,
as silent and industrious
as cilia.

WHAT SONG DO I SING HER?

Most of the love songs I know issued
from white-sheathed throats,
and the hearts they were sung for
were wrapped just the same.

Some of those love songs take place
in our long-ago Toronto,
the home that gathers fresh grief
with each new build on the skyline.

None of the love songs I know can ever
suffice to explain her,
this dark-skinned woman told so often
she's nothing but rage.

All of the love songs that might fit
even my parents don't remember,
only survive now as souvenirs
plundered for white minds.

I don't yet know what song to sing her.
I crane towards a start.

CONCORD & BLOOR

The week after he was struck
and killed by a bus,
we paused at his street-side memorial.
He looked out towards the lake
from his very best photo,
framed by a pool of candles snuffed
by long January nights.

You bent down, my favourite
purple Bic in your hand;
tenderness packed
so densely in your body,
like a mother amongst light poles
in a blizzard of cold wind and passing stares.

BIG

I like elephants. Or I should say I love elephants.
I like that they chew their food slowly the way my little brother does.
I like the way they lumber, not lope.
>The simplicity of their thick bodies.
>How each foot has the girth of a tree.
>How their ears seem almost razor sharp at the edges.
I like that their bodies can produce a substance like ivory.
I like that they take revenge against poachers and murderers.
I like the steel-spring strength hidden under the folds of skin.

I regret being born in this thin, useless body.
I regret these toothpick legs.
I regret this big nose which is somehow not big enough.
I regret this disproportionate brain that has outgrown its empathy.

I regret not being born an elephant
or I could have wrapped my trunk tightly around you
and taken you away from this violence and hate.
I could have moved one thick leg after the other
through the garbage and the scar tissue and the broken bones.

But you are here with your arms wrapped around me.
You are here with your back absorbing the blows.
You are here dying to take revenge.
Maybe you are an elephant.
That is why I love you.

LIKE FRIEDRICH'S WANDERER

The city below Davenport Hill
is eternal.
Even the earth seems built
from blocks of sky.

The clouds—elsewhere heralds
of storm or holy presence—
submit to her,
become nothing but frame.

She turns
and though there's barely a smile
silhouetted against that majesty,
it's enough.

Mama, don't be mad.
All you tried and tried to hammer
through my thick skull
she taught with only a look.

SHE

She who waits at the end of every thought,
occupies every corner.

She who is the ease in all your grins.

She who wakes your pen
from its long, fitful sleep.

Your starting shot,
your finish line made flesh.

She who becomes your silent prayer.

We were all carved from a single soul,
but for eternities your two fragments
clung especially close.

She the mirror
that lays bare every flaw.

She who finally destroys you.

It can be no other way.
Now put yourself back together.

THE FLAW

Islamic tapestries
are purposefully woven with flaws:
errant threads,
failures of symmetry.
Concessions to God
and His singular perfection.
An acquiescence to the fallibility
of even the best.

It should take more than a flaw
to undermine a levee.

But I lack even a carpet's constitution.
One flaw and I come unravelled.
One flaw and it all comes rushing out.

A COURTESY TO A COWARD

It was more than courage
that gave her the strength
to stand before me unflinching.

To tell me she loves me,
then walk away.

The simple turn no one else could make.

POSSESSION

MAJNUN

This is the story of two stars
and the inevitable decay of their orbit.

The slow dawn of reality,
inertia sapped
and thus collision,
shearing matter from both bodies,
setting each back on a lonesome trajectory.
Only his need to salve
the burning brand she left
outstrips self-preservation.
He peels himself from familiar orbits,
hurtles after her into an unknown.

This is the willing dereliction of safety.
The wild chase towards absolution.

But pursuit is so often
a precursor to violence.

PATTERN

Look.
It's been a minute
since I last unravelled,
I know,
but I can
once again dance
alone in my bedroom
and stay with one song for more than five seconds
and tear up during even the sappiest movies
and read for an afternoon uninterrupted
and inspire confidence in my vocation
and resist the urge to hide when a familiar face approaches
and hit friends back within a reasonable time
respond *Good*
and not have it sound like an outright lie
and straighten the worried squiggle of Mama's mouth
and stave off Papa's disappointment
and
and
bnd
bud
but
but
but each night like clockwork
she drives the street sweeper past my door,
picking at the barely mended threads.

SIPPING ZAMZAM WATER IN REGENT PARK

I met her at our old spot, days after she returned from the desert. There was a safety in her, or maybe in those walls, a warmth enough that I could speak: of symptoms at least, if still not a source. So she gave me the sacred water from the Zamzam Well and said:

"Stand up.
Face Qibla.
Take three sips.
Make dua.
Then drink the rest down."

Though there was barely any belief left in this flesh, I wondered could I make more than one prayer. She snorted as if to say: "What? Your health's not enough?"

So I stood up.
Faced Qibla.
Took three sips.

Thought of the family cannibalizing itself in silence. Of this body dissolving. But I must've passed then through some novice gate of love, having seen you when I prayed.

Then drank the rest of the holy water down
and continued on with my day.

APOPHENIA

You appeared
to a chorus of
old men's cracking knees and backs
as we straightened up out of sajdah
at Friday prayer,
your face unmistakable
in the mosaic patterns
on the walls of the masjid.

Day by day, I stayed there gazing,
longing once again
for the sharp lines of your eyes and mouth.

The imam grinned proudly
mistaking my obsession for piety.

Fasted, or maybe just forgot to eat,
until like you, I became
a shadow of lines and angles.

I began to inch my way towards you
on memory's dusty beams.

SLEEPING WITH THE SUN

I wonder if her infidelities
were born from my own reluctance
when I used to treat her like
diabetics treat sugar
and ration myself from her touch.

She's gone again,
left me the jilted
partner to her errant nomad,
deserted with thoughts of her melting
through long black skirts, shrouds, veils.

From this miserable winter,
relay a message:

Tell her I'm nothing without her.
That I'm willing to share.
Tell her I'm ripping down the black curtains
I hung as a ward against her.
I'm opening up the sliding glass door,
standing here on the balcony
like an inverted Juliet
waiting for my Romeo to slink
down her ivied trellis.

AFTERTASTE

You darted between speeding cars,
    danced on the edge of forty-foot drops,
    pirouetted and twirled from police batons.
You forced my fingers deep into this worried mouth,
        acrid from the taste of ten half-chewed nails.
I was too scared to catch you
when you finally fell.

I scrape and scrape
but that bitter flavour
still makes me choke.
Everyone else tastes safe.

DOUBT

It is hydra
of proliferating heads,
forest seeding so fast
it outpaces the burn.
Each branch bends
with the same question:

Did she ever really love you?
Does anyone?

DEATH OF AN ARSONIST

The only belief I've ever held
is in the cleansing power of flame.
The only calm,
the moment before ignition.
But so deep have your tendrils penetrated now,
fire can no longer breathe.

REVULSION

IBN SALAM

This is the story of two stars
and the ever present third,

whose collision with Layla
first sent her hurtling
into Majnun's arms,
the third to whom
she was always fated to return.

This is the surrender to grief.
The ignition of a much greater madness.

Only this Layla wasn't taken
by a cruel, cosmic whim —
she escaped of her own volition.

GRAVITY

An insignificant thing
lacks the needed weight to attract.
Laws state
it will barely inspire a reaction.
An insignificant thing
will always try to accrete,
even if hate is the only available mass.

Let it build
until you collapse alone
beneath your own weight.
Then for a moment
you will become a fire on the horizon,
beautiful
and impossible to ignore.

THE SCREAM

Scream.
Start with yourself:
    Son of a bitch Little bastard
    Worthless piece of shit
    Why the fuck are you even alive
    All the other things your dad said
    You coward You insect
    You little paki bitch
    Knew you couldn't cut it
    Why'd you even bother

Scream.
Turn on them:
    You whore You scumbag
    Especially him
    Didn't I hear his name once
    Wasn't he the shitty ex
    He doesn't even know where he's left me
    An inferno even I can't bear

Scream.
Don't spare God:
    I must be a joke to you
    Why the fuck else would you forsake me in this desert
    Why does their falling in love for a second time
    feel like this?

STARING AT THE SUN

The pupil can only contract so much
before it shuts forever.
The phantom will remain
long after you blink.
They tell you not to stare
because all foolish dares
eventually beget tragedy.
Because pride has always
been deadlier than poison.

What they don't tell you
is that the deepest crevasses
were never meant to be illuminated.
They don't tell you that one day
we will all beg mercy
from the burning blade of memory.

The eyes themselves will become supplicants.
They will strain for any release.

VISION IN THE SANDS

i. gate

these dunes were always my home
i guess i'm through playing otherwise
so familiar
i can traverse them with my eyes closed

but there's still the centre
where even this reckless heart
was never fool enough to go

ii. nexus

here i understand
the childhood fear of quicksand
a memory of terror so immense
it vibrated back from this moment
against the temporal grain

all else here also ignores that intractable law
the sand already glass already mirrors
a single voice
what i am
what i've always been

iii. torture

no more safety
nowhere to hide

nothing left for you now
but to look
at all the charred flesh
you've left in your wake
the still-oozing blisters
across backs
that tried to shield you once
from the hell that is yourself

iv. interrogation

what name befits an insect
inflicting an elephant's violence

what do you call the creature
so twisted by revenge

what else could revolt its own reflection

you've always known the word
just say it
let this sad thing come to an end

v. the sad thing

it's true i begged for this so many times
traced the outline on my skin with a blade
took the slow coward's road towards it with my vices
but now it's close enough to touch
i see it for what it is
what it's always been

faith without salvation
the very void
i've been trying to outrun

only the desert offers no release
parting
hungry
to finally claim its prize

now i am only a muffled scream
raw flesh of a throat being buried
ears straining for any response
but all that comes back is
harsh nothingness
empty echo across sand

vi. this is it

mama
i see now
this foolish son of yours won't survive this centre
he should never have come here

he should've made a home in his sadness
what else could he have expected
when even neruda
a king amongst lovers
was trying to forget

someone
anyone
save me from this now

i promise i'll never slip
i promise to be perfect
if you'll only do me
this one final kindness

this is it
the realization of papa's prophecy
where the beast sees in its reflection
no poet no king no son no lover
and is finally destroyed

please

i'm begging you now
from every cell

don't abandon me here

all i ever wanted
was

THE WORD

THE WORD

THE WORD

THE WORD

LAY YOUR HANDS ON ME

Hazrat Isa returned from the desert,
a word in his hands
with power enough to heal.

Only maybe the word was obscured
by the flourish of scripture,
blurred by the passage of time.
Maybe the word for which
he became custodian was so plain it
hardly merited poetry.

Maybe those carpenter's hands came back
bearing a much simpler message.
One held not only by prophets.
One I'm now ready to receive.

PEACE TREATY

The bodies are buried.
The weapons too,
here where the earth can reclaim them.
The birds have come back—
in their song, a reminder.

I'll spend my days now beneath the boughs,
the weight of an old soldier.
When children come visit
and wonder wide-eyed at my scars,
warn them these aren't medals.

Maybe one day we return here,
by chance or design,
once new life is lush enough to mask.
I greet you this time
alone, unarmed,
with just the more than enough
of this life in my hands.

IRFAAN

means knowledge, that much you'd heard.
But knowledge of exactly what sort?

It's a knowing of God, our daughter told you,
something like nirvana. The love you left behind
in your struggle to adapt.

That same daughter told you love is a mass,
a root sunk deep.

You thought that a threat,
like you thought life a race.
That seed in you
is just now starting to sprout.
Don't hurry love,
this alone is our wish.

SONG MY SISTERS SING ME

Cacophony will always rule here,
that I know won't change.

Only now the demon head
lies cradled in loving hands
and your voices ring the loudest
back across the lake.

DEATH OF CAIN

Cain died at the end of all attempts
to master the laws of reaction.
Cain fell from the sky
on the thrust of his envy.
Cain died on a day just like this.

As death neared
he noticed the fire he wielded
like a torturer's tool
was, in the end, intended for him.

Cain died today
with gratitude on his lips,
for every star whose passing gravity
aligned him
to this final collision.
And even as he burned up
through his last descent,
he didn't doubt the wisdom.

A boy enslaved by his own nature
immolates himself,
then somehow finds his way back.

POPS,

A prophecy visited me once
at the bottom of a coffee cup,
in piles of chicken bones,
telling the oldest story,
the one that came before.

Only reality veered so far from the vision.
No teary regrets,
no threats of perdition,
just the knot in you loose enough
to finally release
the other fathers
I'd never met beneath.

Pops, it was so obvious it seemed absurd,
this cycle of ours—
sons
branding their broken hearts onto sons
like heirlooms.

So Pops, I'm sorry
for ever thinking myself different.
If you'd understand that,
it would be a kind of forgiveness.

MOMS,

I never went past the precipice.
I was standing there forever.

I thought I was trying to spare you from terror,
but the mercy was yours.
The cord never truly severed.

A KNOWING

I only sought cures for the symptoms,
could never acknowledge the source.
That I alone lay beyond the pale of Your love
was the fear driving this arsonist force.

Though a beast I might stay in the eyes of some
for the harm that belief caused,
it's the You now in me I feel steadily blooming
that tells me I'm finally absolved.

In this knowledge there will remain weakness
but never again any doubt.

ARRIVAL

There is the smallest of sounds
like a beetle's clicking mandibles.
A plain breeze from the backyard.

The mirror shifts a fraction of a fraction
and in its new light
I look and, for the first time, see
    both elephant and insect are myself.
    The beauty of the cicada song.
    The cockroach's unbreakable will.

I see
    family
    fraternity
    all creation
    love
    God

Too powerful for a self to overcome.

Ameen.

ACKNOWLEDGMENTS

Thank you first and foremost to the Most High. Thank you to my parents, Najma and Mustafa, for their two vastly different but equally valuable lessons about love. Thank you to Emily Pohl-Weary who first believed in my writing when I didn't myself. Thank you to my editor, Nick Thran, who so expertly mined this collection out of the ore. Thank you to my little brother Rizwan for his phenomenal and beautifully strange cover design. Thank you to Brick Books, the Ontario and Toronto Arts Councils, the Writers' Trust of Canada, the Parkdale Street Writers, and That Lit Salon. Thank you to many others: Asha Jeffers, Kirk Mason, Noor Naga, Imran Ali, Huda Hassan, Chuqiao Yang, Jack Illingworth (for the much-needed encouragement), Shara Temahagali, Pacinthe Mattar, Doyali Islam, Whitney French, Alayna Munce, Robert Priest, George Elliott Clarke, Lawrence Hill, Kendrick Lamar (whose *good kid, m.A.A.d city* album provided the narrative skeleton for this collection), and everyone else who held my hyperemotional ass down over the years.

IRFAN ALI is a poet, essayist, writer, and educator. His short poetry collection, "Who I Think About When I Think About You" was shortlisted for the 2015 Bronwen Wallace Award for Emerging Writers. *Accretion* is his first full-length work. Irfan was born, raised, and still lives in Toronto.